A Special Gift

Presented to:

_____

From:

_____

Date:

_____

A Family Legacy for Your Children

Reflections
from a
Mother's
Heart

Your Life Story in Your Own Words

COUNTRYMAN

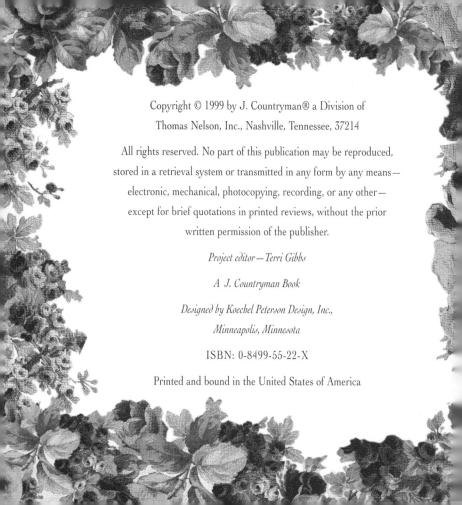

Project editor — Terri Gibbs

A J. Countryman Book

Designed by Koechel Peterson Design, Inc.,
Minneapolis, Minnesota

ISBN: 0-8499-55-22-X

Printed and bound in the United States of America

Contents

Introduction

Days pass…seasons change…months meld into years, and we stand looking back at our lives—childhood memories, exciting moments, crises, and turning points.

In January we think of new beginnings; in February of valentines, first dates, and first kisses. Does ever a June pass without thoughts of our own wedding day? Surely summer evokes backseat memories of seemingly unending trips to grandma's house or the beach. And don't November and December bring to mind family traditions and celebrations held tightly through the years?

Like ivy on the garden trellis, our lives are inescapably entwined with the seasons and months of the year. That is why we have designed this mother's memory journal in a twelve-month format. Each month features several intriguing questions with space to write

a personal answer. Questions explore family history, childhood memories, lighthearted incidents, cherished traditions, and the dreams and spiritual adventures encountered in a lifetime of living.

Whether you choose to complete the journal in a few days, weeks, or over the course of a year, the questions will take you on a journey through the times and seasons of your life. This makes a tangible family record to pass on as a gift to a son or daughter, a loving memoir of written words that are windows to a mother's heart.

No matter what your age, memory and reminiscence open a richer, fuller understanding of who you are as a family. Let this memory journal be a starting point—a door into discussing and sharing the unique qualities of your life. May *Reflections from a Mother's Heart* draw you closer to each other as you share the experiences of a lifetime. 🖎

Personal Portrait

your full given name _____.

your date of birth _____.

your place of birth _____.

your mother's full name _____.

  the place and date of her birth _____.

your father's full name _____.

  the place and date of his birth _____.

the names of your paternal grandparents _____.

  the places and dates of their births _____.

the names of your maternal grandparents _____.

  the places and dates of their births _____.

the names of your siblings _____.

  the places and dates of their births _____.

_____.

_____.

the date and place of your marriage _____.

the full given name of your husband _____.

the names and birth dates of your children _____.

_____.

_____.

What is your favorite?

flower _____.

perfume _____.

color _____.

hymn or song _____.

book _____.

author _____.

Bible verse _____.

dessert _____.

vacation spot _____.

type of food _____.

sport _____.

leisure activity _____.

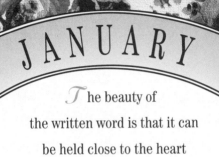

JANUARY

*T*he beauty of
the written word is that it can
be held close to the heart
and read over and over again.

FLORENCE LITTAUER

What was your favorite pastime as a child? Did you prefer doing it alone or with someone else? _____.

_____

_____

_____

_____

_____

_____

_____

_____

_____

_____

_____

Who gave you your name and why? Did you have a family nickname? How did you get it? _____.

_____
_____
_____
_____
_____
_____
_____
_____
_____
_____
_____
_____

Were you baptized or dedicated as an infant? If so, where and by whom?

_____
_____
_____

What kind of prayer did you say before you went to sleep? Who taught you how to pray it?

_____
_____
_____
_____
_____

January

When did you first go to church? What are your earliest memories of church? _____.

_____

_____

_____

_____

_____

_____

_____

_____

_____

_____

_____

*W*here did your father go to work every day and what did he do? _____

_____

_____

_____

_____

_____

*H*ow did your mother spend her day? Did she have a job or do volunteer work outside the home?

_____

_____

_____

_____

_____

_____

January

*List one special
memory about each of
your brothers and sisters.*

_____.

_____.

_____.

_____.

_____.

_____.

_____.

_____.

_____.

_____.

_____.

_____.

*Recall for me some of the most important
lessons you have learned in life:*

_____

_____

_____

_____

_____

_____

_____

_____

_____

_____

_____

FEBRUARY

*F*or all of us,
today's experiences are
tomorrow's memories.

BARBARA JOHNSON

*S*hare a memory of your grandparents or an older person you loved. _____

_____
_____
_____
_____
_____
_____
_____
_____
_____
_____
_____
_____

February

When did you become a Christian? How did your life change? _____
_____
_____
_____
_____
_____
_____
_____
_____
_____
_____
_____
_____

*Who gave you your
first Bible and how old were
you when you received it?
How did it influence your life?*

_____.
_____.
_____.
_____.
_____.
_____.
_____.
_____.
_____.
_____.
_____.
_____.

$\mathcal{W}$*hat chores did you have to do when you were growing up? Did you get an allowance? How much was it?* _____.

$\mathscr{T}$ell me about your first job. _____

_____

_____

_____

_____

_____

_____

_____

_____

_____

_____

_____

_____

_____

_____

MARCH

*T*he mother's heart
is the child's schoolroom.

HENRY WARD BEECHER

*D*id the pastor or a visiting missionary ever come to your house for dinner or tea? Share one vivid experience. _____.

_____
_____
_____
_____
_____
_____
_____
_____
_____
_____
_____

March

*Who was your favorite
teacher? Why?*

_____

_____

_____

_____

_____

_____

_____

_____

_____

_____

_____

_____

_____

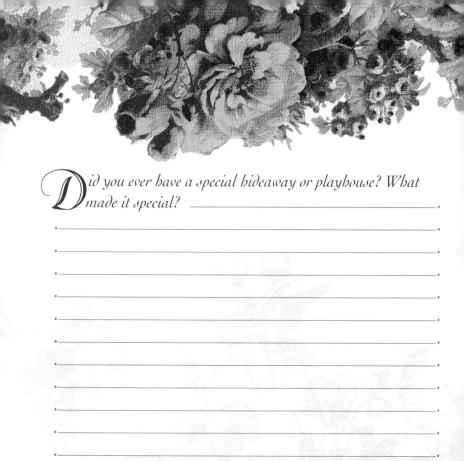

Did you ever have a special hideaway or playhouse? What made it special? _____.

_____
_____
_____
_____
_____
_____
_____
_____
_____
_____
_____

*W*hat extracurricular activities were you involved in during high school? Why did you choose those activities? _____.

_____
_____
_____
_____
_____
_____
_____
_____
_____
_____
_____
_____

March

What crazy fads do you remember in grade school? _____.

_____

_____

_____

_____

_____

_____

_____

_____

_____

_____

_____

March

*W*hat did you do to
celebrate birthdays when
you were growing up?

_____

_____

_____

_____

*T*ell me about your most memorable birthday.

_____

_____

_____

_____

_____

_____

March

Record here some gardening or decorating tips that you have found helpful:

_____

_____

_____

_____

_____

_____

_____

_____

_____

_____

_____

APRIL

*H*owever time or circumstance
may come between a mother and her child,
their lives are interwoven forever.

PAM BROWN

*W*hat were your family finances like when you were growing up? How did that affect you? _____.

April

*D*o you remember your first communion? What influence did it have on you and your family? _____

_____

_____

_____

_____

_____

_____

_____

_____

_____

_____

_____

_____

_____

What mischievous childhood experience do you remember? How did it affect you?

_____
_____
_____
_____
_____
_____
_____
_____
_____
_____
_____
_____
_____

April

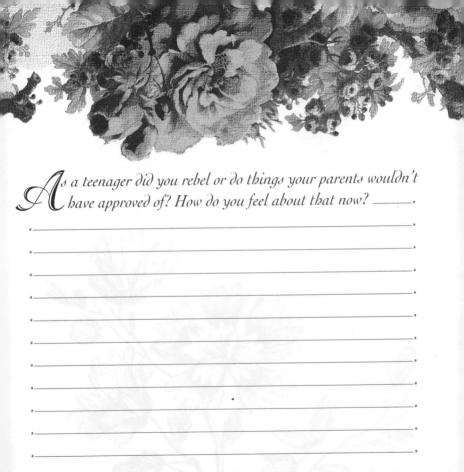

As a teenager did you rebel or do things your parents wouldn't have approved of? How do you feel about that now? _____.

_____
_____
_____
_____
_____
_____
_____
_____
_____
_____
_____

*D*escribe your mother in her best dress. _____.
_____.
•_____.
•_____.
•_____.

•_____.
*D*escribe your father in his working clothes.
_____.
•_____.
•_____.
•_____.
•_____.
•_____.

*What did your family
like to do on weekends?
Describe one particularly
memorable event.*

_____.
_____.
_____.
_____.
_____.
_____.
_____.
_____.
_____.
_____.
_____.
_____.
_____.
_____.

Share one of your mother's best recipes or a recipe for one of your favorite childhood dishes:

_____

_____

_____

_____

_____

_____

_____

_____

_____

_____

MAY

*I*n search of
my mother's garden,
I found my own.

ALICE WALKER

What toys did you like to play with? Why those particular toys? _____

_____

_____

_____

_____

_____

_____

_____

_____

_____

_____

_____

_____

_____

May

How old were you when you understood that God loves you? Recall your early thoughts about God's love. _____.

_____

_____

_____

_____

_____

_____

_____

_____

_____

_____

$\mathcal{D}$id you attend family reunions? Share a memory of one.

May

*Tell about someone who
influenced your life profoundly.*

_____.

_____.

_____.

_____.

_____.

_____.

_____.

_____.

_____.

_____.

_____.

_____.

May

*W*here did you go to grade school? Junior High? High School? Tell me about your best childhood friend. _____.

May

If you went to college or to a career training school, where did you go and why? _____.

_____.

_____.

_____.

_____.

_____.

_____.

_____.

_____.

_____.

_____.

_____.

*What were your
youthful goals and ambitions
for life? Which ones have
you been able to fulfill?*

_____.

_____.

_____.

•_____.

•_____.

•_____.

•_____.

•_____.

•_____.

•_____.

•_____.

•_____.

JUNE

*R*ings and jewels are not gifts,

but apologies for gifts.

The only gift is a portion of thyself.

RALPH WALDO EMERSON

What fashions were popular when you were in high school? Did you like them? Why or why not? _____.

_____

_____

_____

_____

_____

_____

_____

_____

_____

_____

_____

How old were you when you met Dad and what attracted you to him?

_____

_____

_____

_____

_____

_____

_____

_____

_____

_____

_____

*When did you first know
you wanted to marry him?
What made you feel that way?*

_____.

_____.

_____.

_____.

_____.

*Share a memory about the way he proposed to you.*_____.

_____.

_____.

_____.

_____.

_____.

_____.

*T*ell me about your wedding day, from beginning to end. _____.

_____

_____

_____

_____

_____

_____

_____

_____

_____

_____

_____

_____

*W*here did you go on your honeymoon? Share one humorous incident.

_____

_____

_____

_____

_____

_____

_____

_____

_____

_____

_____

_____

*W*hat was your first house or apartment together like?

_____

_____

_____

_____

_____

*D*o you remember one of the meals you fixed after you were married? How has your cooking changed since then?

_____

_____

_____

_____

_____

What do you love best about Dad now?

_____ .
_____ .
_____ .
. _____ .
. _____ .
. _____ .
. _____ .
. _____ .
. _____ .
. _____ .
. _____ .
. _____ .

June

JULY

J look back and see how
I've become who I am by a family
that found sweetness and joy
somewhere inside when . . .
life experience tasted bitter.

KATHY BOICE

*S*hare a family tradition or memory from the Fourth of July.

$\mathcal{D}$id you ever go camping with your family? Where? Record one exceptional camping experience. _____.

_____
_____
_____
_____

_____

$\mathcal{D}$id you learn to swim? _____.
How? _____

_____
_____
_____
_____
_____

*D*id you ever travel abroad? How old were you and where did you go? Did you travel alone or with a group? _____.

_____

_____

_____

_____

_____

*T*ell me about your most memorable trip._____

_____

_____

_____

_____

_____

_____

July

$\mathcal{D}$id your relatives come to visit in the summer or did you go
to visit them? What are your memories of those visits. ____.

_____

_____

_____

_____

_____

_____

_____

_____

_____

_____

*H*ow did you learn to drive? _____

_____

_____

_____

_____

_____

*W*hat was your first car like? _____

_____

_____

_____

_____

_____

*Did a tragedy ever
strike your family?
How were you affected?*

_____.
_____.
_____.
_____.
_____.
_____.
_____.
_____.
_____.
_____.
_____.
_____.
_____.

Share a favorite poem or a passage of writing that has been especially meaningful in your life:

_____

_____

_____

_____

_____

_____

_____

_____

_____

_____

AUGUST

*T*he family—that dear
octopus from whose tentacles
we never quite escape,
nor, in our inmost hearts,
ever quite wish to.

DODIE SMITH

$\mathcal{N}$ame a book or author that helped you develop a philosophy of life. Share some of those insights. _____.

*D*id you have a collection when you were growing up? What initially sparked your interest in it? _____.

_____

_____

_____

_____

_____

_____

_____

_____

_____

_____

_____

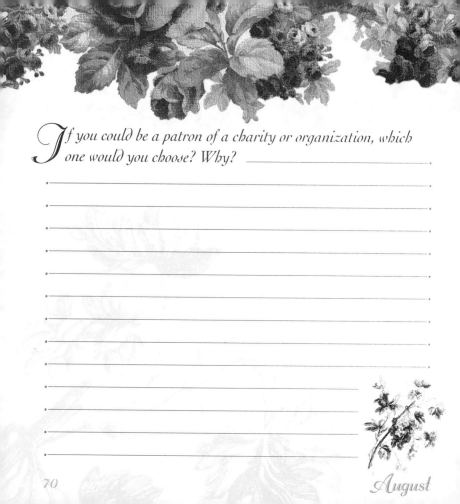

If you could be a patron of a charity or organization, which one would you choose? Why?

70

August

When did you learn how to ride a bike, or to water ski, snow ski, roller skate, or sail? Share your memories of the experience.

*D*escribe a frightening or difficult experience from childhood. How did you respond to it? _____.

· _____.
· _____.
· _____.
· _____.
· _____.
· _____.
· _____.
· _____.
· _____.
· _____.
· _____.
· _____.
· _____.
· _____.

August

What summer games and activities did your family enjoy?

_____

_____

_____

_____

_____

_____

What was your favorite activity? _____

_____

_____

_____

_____

_____

Tell me about your most unforgettable summer experience as a child.

_____.
_____.
_____.
_____.
_____.
_____.
_____.
_____.
_____.
_____.
_____.
_____.

August

SEPTEMBER

*O*ur lives are a
mosaic of little things, like putting
a rose in a vase on the table.

INGRID TROBISCH

Tell about a special outing you took with your mother or your father. _____

_____

_____

_____

_____

_____

_____

_____

_____

_____

_____

_____

_____

September

What was your favorite subject in grade school, junior high, and high school? What was your major in college? Why?

_____.
_____.
_____.

._____.
._____.
._____.
._____.
._____.
._____.
._____.
._____.

September

As a young person did you volunteer for work in church, community, or social services? Tell me about it. _____.

_____

_____

_____

_____

_____

_____

_____

_____

_____

_____

_____

_____

_____

September

*W*hen did you move away from home? Describe where you lived and how you felt about it. _____.

•_____•
•_____•
•_____•
•_____•
•_____•
•_____•
•_____•
•_____•
•_____•
•_____•
•_____•

*W*ho was your best friend after you were married? Describe some of the fun things you did together. _____.

_____
_____
_____
_____
_____
_____
_____
_____
_____
_____
_____
_____

What are your spiritual strengths?

_____

_____

_____

_____

_____

How would you like to grow spiritually? _____

_____

_____

_____

_____

_____

September

*W*hat special talents did your parents nurture in you? How have you developed those talents? _____.

_____

_____

_____

_____

_____

*W*hat would you still like to learn to do? Why? _____.

_____

_____

_____

_____

_____

OCTOBER

"*H*ow will our children know
who they are if they don't know
where they came from?"

Ma in *Grapes of Wrath*

What Bible verse or Scripture puzzles you the most? Which blesses you the most? Why?

————————————————.

————————————————.

————————————————.

•————————————————.

•————————————————.

•————————————————.

•————————————————.

•————————————————.

•————————————————.

•————————————————.

•————————————————.

84

October

Have you ever been in an accident, had surgery or a long illness? Tell me about it. ———————————,

_____

_____

_____

_____

_____

_____

_____

_____

_____

_____

_____

*W*hat responsibilities did your parents require of you as a child? Explain how this affected your growth and development.

$\mathcal{N}$ame your favorite hobby. When and where did you start doing it? Why do you enjoy it?

When and where did you buy your first house? Describe the house and explain any significance it held for you.

October

Did you ever go on a hayride or bob for apples? Tell about fun harvest activities you enjoyed with other young people. ———

———————————————————————————————————

———————————————————————————————————

———————————————————————————————————

———————————————————————————————————

———————————————————————————————————

———————————————————————————————————

———————————————————————————————————

———————————————————————————————————

———————————————————————————————————

———————————————————————————————————

———————————————————————————————————

———————————————————————————————————

Share some helpful home remedies or tips for good health:

_____

_____

_____

_____

_____

_____

_____

_____

_____

_____

_____

NOVEMBER

*I*n our family an experience was not finished, not truly experienced, unless written down or shared with another.

ANNE MORROW LINDBERGH

What individuals have had the greatest impact on your spiritual life? How did they impact your life? _____.

November

What is your most vivid memory of being pregnant?

_____.
_____.
_____.
_____.
_____.
_____.
_____.
_____.
_____.
_____.
_____.
_____.

*H*ow did you choose my name and why? _____.

_____.
_____.
_____.
_____.
_____.
_____.
_____.

*W*hat is your most poignant memory about my childhood?

_____.
_____.
_____.
_____.
_____.
_____.

November

$\mathcal{W}$hat was a favorite Thanksgiving tradition in your family? _____.

_____
_____
_____
_____
_____
_____
_____
_____
_____
_____
_____
_____

*What are some things
from your childhood
that you are thankful for?*

_____ .
_____ .
_____ .
_____ .
_____ .
_____ .
_____ .
_____ .
_____ .
_____ .
_____ .
_____ .
_____ .

November

*W*hat family custom would you like to pass on to your children and grandchildren?

_____

_____

_____

_____

_____

_____

_____

_____

_____

_____

_____

What new tradition would you like to start in the family? What is its significance?

_____.
_____.
_____.
_____.
_____.
_____.
_____.
_____.
_____.
_____.
_____.
_____.

November

DECEMBER

*I*f everything special and warm and
happy in my formative years could
have been consolidated into one word,
that word would have been *Christmas.*

GLORIA GAITHER

Tell about some Christmas rituals in your family and how you felt about them. _____

_____

_____

_____

_____

_____

_____

_____

_____

_____

_____

_____

_____

_____

December

*W*hat favorite Christmas treasures have you kept from year to year? Share their origins. _____

_____

_____

_____

_____

_____

_____

_____

_____

_____

_____

_____

What is your favorite Christmas carol? Why? _____

_____
_____
_____
_____
_____
_____
_____
_____
_____
_____
_____
_____
_____
_____

Describe the Christmas that has been the most meaningful to you.

_____

_____

_____

_____

_____

_____

_____

_____

_____

_____

_____

_____

What would be the most wonderful gift you could receive? Why?

_____.
_____.
_____.
_____.
_____.
_____.
_____.
_____.
_____.
_____.
_____.

December

Tell me about a time when God answered a specific prayer for you.

_____

_____

_____

_____

_____

_____

_____

_____

_____

_____

_____

_____

_____

Share a favorite Thanksgiving or
Christmas recipe:

_____
_____
_____
_____
_____
_____
_____
_____
_____
_____
_____

What advice about life do you want others to remember?

_____

_____

_____

_____

_____

_____

_____

_____

_____

_____

Share some insights from Scripture that have guided your spiritual journey:

_____

_____

_____

_____

_____

_____

_____

_____

_____

_____

_____

_____

What has been the happiest time of your life?

_____

_____

_____

_____

_____

_____

_____

_____

_____

_____

What word best describes your life?
Explain why:

_____

_____

_____

_____

_____

_____

_____

_____

_____

_____

Photos

Photos

Send for your FREE Gift Book Catalog!

Preview the J. Countryman gift book line in our new catalog sent to you at NO cost. These beautifully bound books represent premium quality at exceptional values. Return this card today to receive your FREE catalog featuring the full line of J. Countryman inspirational gift books, devotional journals, leather-bound daily planners and other quality gifts. Simply complete the information below and drop this postage paid card in the mail.

Name _____

Address_____

City _____ ST _____ Zip _____

Phone (_____)_____

Church Name _____

E-Mail Address _____

Priority Code: 07126